GW00501366

MYSTERIES in the DEVON LANDSCAPE

HILARY WREFORD and MICHAEL WILLIAMS

BOSSINEY BOOKS

First published in 1985
by Bossiney Books,
St Teath, Bodmin, Cornwall.

Typeset, printed and bound in Great Britain
by A. Wheaton & Co., Exeter.

All rights reserved
© Hilary Wreford and Michael Williams 1985
ISBN 0 948158 05 0

ABOUT THE AUTHORS — AND THE BOOK

Hilary Wreford is a Devonian, a Capricorn subject born at Brixham. She trained as a nurse and now operates as a part-time community nurse in and around Okehampton. She has contributed features on Dartmoor subjects to both *The Okehampton Times* and *The Tavistock Times*, has done research for three Bossiney titles, and in 1984 made her debut as a Bossiney author in *Strange Somerset Stories*, writing about 'Some Somerset Curiosities'.

Early in 1985 Hilary Wreford contributed a chapter to *Westcountry Mysteries*, introduced by Colin Wilson: Double Mystery at Hatherleigh. Here, with Michael Williams, she explores *Mysteries in the Devon Landscape*.

A Cornishman, Michael Williams started full-time publishing in 1975. With his wife Sonia, he runs Bossiney Books from a cottage and converted barn in North Cornwall – they are literally cottage publishers, specialising in Westcountry subjects by Westcountry authors. For ten years they ran the Bossiney House Hotel, outside Tintagel – hence Bossiney Books.

Outside publishing and writing, Michael Williams is a keen cricket enthusiast and collector of cricket books. He is President of the Cornish Crusaders Cricket Club, and a member of the Cornwall and Gloucestershire County Clubs. He is also a member of the RSPCA and has actively worked for reform in laws relating to animal welfare. Recently he was elected to the Ghost Club.

Of *Mysteries in the Devon Landscape* the authors reflect, 'Nearly all the places featured have a strong, sometimes strangely magnetic quality. We felt we had to go to such sites – or include them. In a curious way, they almost picked themselves. Generally, we have been drawn to places that either have a good tale or a strong atmosphere – or fire speculation.'

Almost all the illustrations here were especially commissioned for this Bossiney title, many showing facets of the Devon landscape rarely seen on the published page.

Introduction

On this journey across the varied acres of Devon, we are looking at the mysteries in the landscape.

In our exploration we have often been compelled to think about some of the unwritten chunks of Devon's long past. Among the strange shapes which people the Devon landscape we have found elements of the Supernatural, entered areas of speculation and among the legends, more than once, have wondered whether there can be such a thing as pure myth. These then are only some of the ingredients that help to create the essential – mysterious Devon.

At the outset we went to the *Collins English Dictionary* for definitions of *mystery* and found as many as three which applied to our expedition:
1. An unexplained or inexplicable event, phenomenon etc.
2. A person or thing that arouses curiosity or suspense because of an unknown, obscure, or enigmatic quality.
3. The state or quality of being obscure, inexplicable or enigmatic.

Consequently ours is a wide umbrella. In fact, some of our subjects are more curiosities than mysteries. But any imaginative traveller across Devon will quickly discover the two are often closely related. Moreover, many of the places featured automatically fan imagination *and* curiosity.

What's around the next corner? Or over that hill?

As a pair of travellers we like to think we're reasonably balanced – and committed – one, a Devonian born and bred, the other Cornish but with some Devon blood in the family tree – and both aware of the magnetism of Devon.

Nearly all the places featured here have a strong, sometimes strangely magnetic quality. We felt we had to go to such sites – or include them. In a curious way, they almost picked themselves.

Right: **'Among the strange shapes that people the Devon landscape we have found elements of the Supernatural . . .'**

Generally we have been drawn to places that either have a good tale or a strong atmosphere – or fire speculation. A number of the sites have a combination of all three ingredients. Devon is, in fact, a mine of myth and folklore, and myth, down the ages, has been the inspiration of some great story-telling.

Friend and fellow Bossiney author Sally Jones in her *Legends of Devon* asked, 'Are legends idle fancy or the high water mark of history, the residue of ancestral memories left after the tide of history has receded?'

We don't pretend to have produced the answer to that big question but we have come to understand the curious fact that sheer history and legend are often intermingled.

Maybe it is not just the place. Perhaps people come into the reckoning too.

Sally Jones, introducing her Legends, reflected: 'It is the live soul of the Devon people, superstitious, hero-worshipping, imaginative, that informs the legends, making them more than half-remembered history or the remnants of folk-memory.' And she brought that same Introduction thoughtfully, eloquently to this close: 'So the legends have become part of the Devon landscape, but the greatest can stand apart, both from the events that engendered them and the stones that preserve their memory, holding their own as magical examples of the story-teller's art, as durable and timeless as the Dartmoor tors.'

This was not intended to be a guidebook, but before many pages had been shaped, before many sites had been visited, we discovered it *could* be just that for some people. But a few words of warning at this early stage. If you are truly searching for mysteries in the Devon landscape, then walking is frequently essential, and, as far as Dartmoor is concerned, riding on horseback remains the best form of transport. There is a rich diversity in this landscape of Devon. Arthur Mee, that master traveller and writer, touring Devon in the 1930s, said, 'She is a mighty county in spirit and size; there are only two counties in England with more acres . . . We may stand on a hundred heights in Devon and look out on scenes as impressive as any in our land.'

Fifty years on, there have, of course, been many changes in some areas. But often on our travels we have remembered his words and realised that what he said remains essentially true – as if he had written those lines only last evening.

Hopefully this combination of words and pictures will provide a kind of map of Mysterious Devon. Of course it's not comprehensive – preference and prejudice have often been our guide – and anyway an all-embracing map of mysteries across the county would have needed a thousand pages.

Everything here is factual – even the legends in the sense that they have been passed on from one generation to another. Writing, however, cannot always be 100 per cent truth even when we say 'This is a myth'. Writing, as that fine American author Truman Capote once recalled, 'can never be altogether pure – nor can the camera, for after all art is not distilled water: personal perceptions, pre-

Right: **'There is a rich diversity in this landscape of Devon.'**

judices, one's sense of selectivity pollute the purity of germless truth.'

We are especially pleased with the illustrations inside these pages. Nearly all of them have been commissioned, a good percentage showing facets of the Devon landscape rarely seen on the published page.

As co-authors, we are indebted to all who have provided such sensitive illustrations and have trekked so many miles to get them – some in the depths of winter across beautiful but difficult Dartmoor.

Felicity Young's drawings of three favourite Dartmoor subjects were commissioned for a good reason. We wanted to see what this talented young Tintagel painter would find – for she was entering 'foreign country'. Dartmoor inevitably has produced most of the mysteries – inevitably because it is a beautiful mysterious world of its own. Even in this, the last quarter of the twentieth century, parts of the Moor can seem more remote, more mysterious than outer space.

Hilary Wreford at 'The Honest Man'. The intriguing question remains: 'Why the Honest Man?' One local character is convinced he knows the answer. In his opinion a traveller — perhaps a miner because the mines were once living things hereabouts — took rather too much liquid refreshment in a Sticklepath inn and later in the evening, resuming his journey, completely lost his bearings. Trying to find someone to direct him in the darkness, he came upon the stone and in his confused state threw his arms around the stone, asking it 'Be you an honest man?' And from that night on, the Sticklepath Stone became 'The Honest Man'.

The photographs that follow are among some of the finest achieved in more than one hundred Bossiney titles.

The camera does quite a few things. It can interpret and record. It can probe a subject deeply or skim a surface. It can distort or be a most honest witness.

It has many talents, but everything depends on the man or woman holding the camera, and we are indeed fortunate to have such a team bringing together this rich Devon harvest.

We feel we must pay special tribute to Mary Lou North, who lives on Dartmoor, and, at very short notice, agreed to take the great majority of photographs for this book.

Mary Lou not only loves and understands Dartmoor, she has captured and frozen some mysterious magical moments. 'Every picture tells a story' may sound rather old hat, yet many that follow do precisely that.

Moreover, in many instances, we like to think that we have broken new ground. Until this exploration, for example, we have never seen pictures of that curious tombstone in Lydford Churchyard or the view from that white rock from which the great John Wesley preached or Bradford Pool.

Tree bole at Waddicombe. Fascinating whichever way you look at it.

Riding is still the best way to see the Moor.

'We have been drawn to places that have a strong
atmosphere . . . '

Wistman's Wood

Woods can be mysterious places, and one of the most mysterious in all Devon is Wistman's Wood on Dartmoor. There is something ominous, threatening in the very name.

Trees have personalities of their own. Some people claim to find great healing energy from them. By simply leaning against a tree, some say they feel better, their energy flow suddenly strengthening.

If trees could talk, we wonder what these at Wistman's Wood would tell us. We shall never know, but we did the next best thing and asked a lady with – we think – considerable gifts to pay a visit here – to find out what she could pick up in the ether.

Shirley Wallis, who lives in Plymstock, is an astrologer and student of psycho-expansion and healing. Psycho-expansion claims to have the ability to go back or forward in time – Shirley went back and this is what she told us.

'Prior to my visit, I researched this place using the technique of psycho-expansion where I enter into a state of heightened consciousness allowing the mind to travel where directed, to view and research the area in question. For about eight minutes I noted my impressions. I have never visited these woods before, and the exercise was done two days previous to my setting off. I was able to "view" Wistman's Wood from above, as if in an aircraft, as well as pick up various vibrations in the area, and immediately made notes of my findings as follows:

' "Somehow, the woods are set upon granite, and there is a seam of quartz running through the centre underground. This makes for great sensitivity in centring the energy field. It has an inverted force field – whatever that means – but in my layman's understanding, Wistman's Wood contains its own heightened awareness due to the centring of energies invisible to the naked eye, but visible to me through psycho-expansion as two spirals set side by side moving in opposite directions. This gave me the distinct impression that the whole place was enclosed and parcelled up so to speak."

'I then moved back in time to the period between 400 and 500 AD enquiring as to who may have been

Wistman's Wood.

in this place: "Used by Mithraic/Druidic people as a purifying centre where much good was wrought. A spring of water is tumbling over rocks through the trees down to a river. Only certain people are allowed here. Their energy fields or vibrations are 'in tune' with the surroundings. It is very isolated, like a world within our world. I received another distinct impression that there is nothing 'wrong' with Wistman's Wood. The unusual feeling that my mind senses can be described as being absorbed by the area when amongst the trees giving a mysterious quality as if harbouring a secret."

'My visit two days later on a bright and breezy afternoon was fascinating. I was surprised at seeing so many granite boulders among the trees, and as I entered the woods I became conscious of a feeling of being "wrapped around". I sat for a while on a boulder observing my surroundings realising that its uniqueness was geographical, geological, mineral and magnetic. Moving on, I came to an upright stone and leaned against it receiving a strong gravitational pull rooting my feet to the spot. Physically, I felt relaxed, peaceful and rather tired, concluding that this was due to the walk necessary to reach the location; however, as I came into a clearing, this feeling immediately lifted, only to return when moving back among the trees. It was then I noticed that the clearing divided Wistman's Wood into two groves side by side, and the impression of a quartz seam I had "seen" through psycho-expansion underground and running through the centre of the area, was through this clearing between one grove and the other, for I came upon one large stone with a surface of quartz. Moving into the second grove of trees, I

'The woods are set upon granite . . .'

noticed a subtle difference in the effect upon my own force field, rather milder and more uplifting. I felt as if there was a positive and negative flow side by side in these two groves of trees.

'I conclude that this place will react upon visitors in a variety of ways according to their own personal energies or force fields, for Wistman's Wood contains its own ability to evolve through time absorbing mysteries and memories, as I was absorbed when there. Once I had left, walking over the Moor homeward, I felt refreshed and full of energy perhaps having experienced the purifying agent used long ago. Others have different experiences through the memories locked there . . . '

Hound Tor

We rate Hound Tor one of the most majestic sights on Dartmoor. It has an element of mystery too. On some days Hound Tor has a genuinely eerie quality, but we have invariably found it a location for recharging the batteries. Therefore we were surprised to read of it in Antony D. Hippisley Coxe's *Haunted Britain* as 'a place which a number of people find unbearable. Some who have tried to overcome their inexplicable fear, have fallen into a trance . . .'

Once more we asked Shirley Wallis to help us by going back in time, and these were her findings.

'Again, using the psycho-expansion technique to investigate before visiting this tor, I made a few notes of my impressions, but found the exercise more difficult since the message was that animal vibrations interfere with everything here, and I could not seem to get a "fix" as it were upon the area. There seemed no positive link to other tors in the vicinity, and yet it looked from above when "viewing", as having been a rather important centre in times gone by.

'My visit to this imposing pile of granite coincided with superb weather and visibility. Once there, I received several impressions. This place had indeed been very active, for in the large area between the two great piles of granite, I "saw" first of all, a settlement of people and animals, and then later, it became a collecting point or shelter, somehow fenced off at either end, full of various animals, but perhaps primarily a kind of small long-haired horse. There were dogs which seemed rather large and absurd in comparison with the size of the horses. No wonder now at the animal vibrations I had picked up through psycho-expansion!

'The granite displayed a bland feeling to my touch

15

– peaceful and agricultural. The whole area had been well populated at one time, and concerned in particular with animal husbandry. While at Hound Tor I was able to relax and easily pick up my favourite time for investigation – the so-called Dark Ages. It seemed the tribes here were animal traders with a gentler nature than I have noted before.

'To me, Hound Tor proved to be a delightful, protective place, still minding its own business and memories.'

Below: **Hound Tor on a May morning.** *Right:* **Felicity Young's interpretation of Hound Tor.**

MDL-B

The Scorhill Stone Circle

The Scorhill Stone Circle, near Gidleigh, is one of the great mysteries of the Devon landscape. Samuel Rowe, who came here in the 1840s, described it as 'by far the finest example of rude but venerable shrines of Druidic worship in Devonshire'.

Mr Rowe, of course, was quite wrong about

Two views of the Scorhill Stone Circle.

Druidic involvement. James Mildren in *Dartmoor in the Old Days* reflected:'. . . but it may have been the scene of ceremonies, possibly sepulchral in nature, and reminiscent of early Bronze Age ritual.'

The fact is stone circles remain tantalizing puzzles, and strange things happen in and around them.

History can tell us very little about these colonies of stone. Through the centuries a variety of suggestions have been made about their origin and purpose; monuments, temples and areas for astrologers are just three of the most popular speculations. Scholars have researched deeply and diligently but the stones retain their ancient secrets, incredibly defying all certain human explanation.

We have heard some eerie accounts about the Scorhill Circle having a strange frightening influence on horses. There have been stories of riders unable to get their horses along the track that winds through this circle of stone. Some animals have shown such a reluctance to enter the circle that their riders have had to make a definite detour. Maybe horses have psychic powers, because in another case we were told of horses behaving out of character in a haunted wood. The wood, on private property, positively terrified some animals; so much so that the owner, though confirming the fact, asked us not to reveal the identity of the location.

In other days horse brasses were regarded as amulets, protecting the animal from the Evil Eye. It's an old country tradition that horses were especially vulnerable to witchcraft. Romanies have always regarded a white horse as a good omen, and horse shoes have long led the field in the realm of charms. Finding a horse shoe is still rated by many as a lucky event, and the great Admiral Nelson is reputed to have nailed one to the mainmast of HMS *Victory*.

Times were when the old folk came to circles, like

'Finding a horse shoe is still rated by many as a lucky event . . .'

this, and performed a very specific ritual. They walked around the circle nine times, firmly believing it would bring them good luck or, at least, protect them from any ill-wishing.

On the subject of stone circles in general, one of the most interesting experiences we heard about concerned Tom Lethbridge, a great seeker after Truth, when he visited the Merry Maidens down in West Cornwall.

Lethbridge maintained that 'the world beyond our world' – a world that can be detected by a pendulum of more than forty inches – consists of vibrations which are four times faster than ours. He further reasoned that the other self can, in fact, answer questions by means of the pendulum.

In this Cornish field near Lamorna, Lethbridge held a pendulum over one of the ancient stones and asked its age. Placing one hand on the stone, he experienced something he described as 'a mild electric shock'.

We heard another interesting case of where a Westcountry farmer had started removing stones from an ancient circle on his land, when he was suddenly taken seriously ill. Local people darkly hinted, 'It's the stones getting back at him . . .' Anyway the idea of moving the stones was finally dropped, but the farmer never fully recovered his health.

'Maybe horses have psychic powers . . .'

Nine Maidens

Another colony of standing stones is to be found near Belstone: referred to by some as the Nine Stones and by others as the Nine Maidens. According to ancient Devon folklore they dance at twelve noon. Our visit was timed to coincide with the magical hour, but, to our disappointment, there was no movement as a cold wind sent an invisible knife across the landscape.

Folk in earlier generations though were certain such stones moved of their own accord – without human or mechanical aid – and we wondered whether their reluctance to 'perform' that day had something to do with modern cynicism.

The fact is these stones are clusters of atoms and molecules – just as we human beings are – and who knows possibly as our human bodies renew parts maybe these old weatherbeaten stones do just the same. So when we talk of 'growing stones' or 'moving stones' we are conceivably clutching at the last remnants of ancient knowledge and culture – in the field of earth currents and their effects on stones.

Colin Wilson, writing in *Westcountry Mysteries*, pondered: 'Why is it that the Westcountry has stronger links with the past than other regions of Britain?

A rationalist would attribute it to the barren moorlands and lonely beaches, often lashed by storms – in other words, to the isolation that stimulates the imagination to produce tales of the mysterious and supernatural. I believe this explanation too simple. As absurd as it sounds, I have come to believe that the explanation lies somehow in the *earth itself*.'

On the subject of 'the electrical field of the earth', Colin Wilson wrote: 'For some reason, certain places have a far stronger field than others. If I walk up Glastonbury Tor, in Somerset, with a plastic dowsing rod in my hands, it twists up and down with a strength and persistence that makes my fingers tired. My wife, who is a far better dowser than I am, found that the "field" of the Tor made her feel sick.'

We felt 'good' here at Belstone, and remembered Rudyard Kipling's words: '. . . the mysterious earth-currents which thrill the clay of our bodies . . .'

It is interesting to think that when Kipling, who had spent many years in the East, made his very first visit to Batemans, the seventeenth-century house that became his Sussex home, he reacted warmly and positively: 'We entered and found her spirit, her *fang shui* – to be good.'

There is a curiously mysterious feature about our photographs of the Nine Maidens. The first, on the left, taken by Ray Bishop in 1982 clearly shows no stone in the centre of the circle, whereas the picture overleaf taken by Mary Lou North three years later reveals a stone, supported by smaller stones occupying the central position. Michael Williams, who appears in the 1982 picture, says emphatically, 'There was no such stone inside the circle that day. A fact Ray Bishop can confirm; and we know because I'm the figure Ray photographed standing inside the circle.' Hilary Wreford is equally emphatic. She and her husband visited the Nine Maidens in May 1985 and she says, 'We both saw the stone standing in the centre as Mary Lou has photographed it. In fact, we handled the stone and thought it somewhat precarious.'

23

Bowerman's Nose

Bowerman's Nose on the eastern flank of Dartmoor has inspired some vivid descriptions. Arthur Mee, on a visit to Devon in the 1930s, reflected that it looked 'for all the world like a good-humoured man in a cardinal's hat'.

Sally Jones, travelling across Dartmoor, only a few years ago, researching for her *Legends of Devon* wrote: 'The weathered granite formation is unmistakable, for seen from one angle it resembles the profile of a man with a huge bulbous nose, like two potatoes, rearing forty feet above the boulders and outcrops, scattered over the slope. As usual the etymologists have a stuffy explanation for the origin of its name, claiming that Bowerman is a corruption of the Celtic *veor maen* or great stone. I prefer the local version, that a man called Bowerman lived at Hound Tor around 1066, and sported a nose identical to the splendidly stubby organ that still adorns the granite column.'

Here at Bowerman's Nose we enter an area of speculation. Some of the old people genuinely believed this strange stone structure was related to The Cheesewring on Bodmin Moor, maintaining they were the remains of massive interconnected power temples, the Cornish temples being dedicated to the well-being of the body whereas their Devon counterparts were for revitalizing the spirit.

These stones on Dartmoor have a good feel, and some visitors claim to feel better for being here. Some may simply say, 'That's the natural healing power of the Moor.' Others, cynics, will suggest the power of auto-suggestion.

Either way, Bowerman's Nose remains a weird and wonderful shape – and a genuine Dartmoor puzzle.

Carrington, an early nineteenth-century poet, described it in verse in 1826 as:

A granite God . . .
To whom in days long flown the suppliant knee
In trembling homage bowed . . .

Dartmoor challenges us, especially our mind and our eyes. Somebody once said Dartmoor taps insistently 'at the door of human curiosity', and Bowerman's Nose is such a challenge.

The novelist Eden Phillpotts, who loved and understood the Moor, once wrote: 'The challenge of Dartmoor is severe indeed, for here conditions and quality of light vary from hour to hour . . .'

In his Dartmoor novel *The River*, he described the Moor brilliantly, memorably: 'Vastness of dominion and transparent purity of light marked that sunset spectacle. Westward the blue sky faded into green, then brightened to pale gold. Each great hill took the purple shadow of its neighbour, each tor and lofty cairn beamed tenderly with rosy fire, then sank and died away into the oncoming gloom.'

Many literary critics today would dismiss such words as 'overwriting' and they may have a point, but you can bring a dozen people to Dartmoor and get twelve totally different reactions. This landscape works on us individually and places, like Bowerman's Nose, do challenge us.

Analysts may analyse, critics may criticise but

when it comes down to it, the value – the importance
– of art for each and every one of us is in what a work
actually *does* for us.

The paintings and drawings of Felicity Young
reveal sharp detail. In her art, we often see more than
when we are physically on site. But it's deeper than
meticulous attention to detail, she manages to evoke
the spirit of the place. Her drawing of Bowerman's
Nose is a good example. Here there is a timeless
quality in the stone shape and the lonely terrain and,
as with some of Dame Barbara Hepworth's sculpture,
you want to handle these ancient stones. For all the
detail of Bowerman's Nose though, or maybe because
of it, Felicity manages to stir our curiosity. 'What is it?
Why here?'

Felicity, who lives at Tintagel and has a studio
there works principally in water colours. We asked
her about her first impressions of Dartmoor – the
impact the Moor had made on the painter inside her.

'I didn't know how I could describe the over-
whelming feeling of emptiness and the sheer sense of
space which exists there. Each rock formation seems
to cry out for my attention, making me wonder how it
was created and how long it had stood with stones
precariously perched. The Moor is full of inspiration
with its evocative scenery and magnificent natural
sculptures. I found myself drawn to these powerful
shapes and the stark beauty of the landscape.'

Bowerman's Nose drawn by Felicity Young.

26

Kitty Jay's Grave

The life of Kitty Jay was a tragic one from beginning to end, and even in death she remains something of a Dartmoor mystery.

Kitty was born an orphan in the eighteenth century. She was sent to work on a farm on the Moor. There she was seduced by a farmer's son and then rejected. Carrying his child, she hanged herself in a barn, seeing no other solution to her problems.

No suicide could be buried on consecrated land. So the first available crossroads became her burial place. In those superstitious days suicides were regarded as potential vampires who might 'walk'.

You'll find her grave set back from the road above Manaton, between Heatree Cross and Swallerton Gate: a grassy mound with a raised foot and headstone.

The perceptive Colin Wilson in *Westcountry Mysteries* 'noticed that crossroad is actually a *trivium* – one of the arms of the crossroad is merely a footpath that goes on to the Moor and leads nowhere. Several people claim to have seen ghosts in the area – as it is noted by Peter Underwood in his *Gazeteer of British Ghosts*. Was Kitty buried at a *trivium* to make sure her spirit went down to the "underworld" and stayed there? If so perhaps the ceremony may not have been wholly successful . . .'

The element of mystery deepened in that Kitty's grave is never minus fresh flowers. We have journeyed past the grave dozens of times and have never found it otherwise. Furthermore you cannot get a local person to 'name' the provider of these floral tributes to Kitty.

We know of one curious character who spent hours in watch, hoping to catch a glimpse of the source of supply, but not once did he see anyone approach the roadside grave with flowers or apparently the intention of laying flowers.

Some say the custom was started during the lifetime of the author Beatrice Chase at her instigation, but who carries on the tradition today is seemingly a closely guarded secret.

Our interest in Kitty Jay was heightened in 1978 through a Westward TV programme featuring Joe Keeton, a Liverpool hypnotist, and Pauline McKay, a pretty dark-haired nurse in her early twenties – Colin Wilson also took part in the programme.

It had all begun when Pauline, under hypnosis upcountry, recalled a previous life as Kitty Jay – someone Pauline had never heard of in this life.

In front of television cameras in Plymouth, Pauline, visiting the region for the first time in her life, was regressed first by Joe Keeton back to her childhood in Devon as Kitty Jay and then questioned by Kay Avila, the interviewer.

In his book *Poltergeist!* Colin Wilson recalled: '. . . it was astonishing to see the nurse suddenly "become" a little girl. If she was faking, she must have been a first-class actress.'

During regression, Pauline told Joe Keeton her name was Kitty Jay, and answering Kay Avila, at one point, the nurse said she was 'ten years old and lived in a big house near "Chagiford" – the old local pronunciation of Chagford – apparently the local orphanage or poor house. Taken forward to her fifteenth birthday, she explained she was now working at a farm near Manaton, and that she had struck

Maggie Ginger and Meridian visiting Kitty Jay's grave.

up a relationship with a man called Rob who worked at Canna Farm. She went on to identify local places like Fingle Bridge and the River Teign and recalled walking with Rob to "the stones" – presumably standing stones which are in the area.

Taken forward in time again, she said she had run away from the farm – at Rob's suggestion – and was living in a remote cottage without furniture. She was very hungry – Rob had promised to stay with her and supply her with food – but he had not kept his word. In Colin Wilson's words: 'She said her stomach hurt, but it was not clear whether this was hunger, or pains connected with pregnancy. Asked to describe Rob's last visit to her, she made it clear that he had insisted on making her lie on the floor to have sex, and that she objected. Finally, Keeton took her forward to her suicide on Canna Farm – she had obviously gone there, hoping to see Rob; it was late afternoon. Her misery and despair were painful to watch, as she described her decision to kill herself. As she began to choke and gasp, Joe soothed her, then woke her up.

'The whole thing was astonishingly convincing – doubly so, since Pauline had never visited the Westcountry before, and had only travelled down that morning.'

Adventure

Walking the moor can be a great adventure. One man who knows it well is Clive Gunnell of Tavistock. Here he is describing a walk with his dog Thurber in *My Dartmoor* which Bossiney published in 1977, now out of print.

'My companion is well ahead of me, every fibre of her being glowing with animal content at the freedom of the morning, snuffling and sniffing at tuft and burrow, shooting away like "a long dog" at the slightest whisper and in mock panic jack-knifing backwards to return and apologise for forgetting me. Without warning, meadow pipits rise skywards from the heather, alarmed at her approach, their strident "pheet" striking discord at the silence until, at the peak of their climb, they glide earthwards triple-tonguing in perfect harmony.

'The sun hidden behind the western heights at day's beginning climbs slowly above Brent Moor, burning off the shadows clinging to the sheltered slopes in a blanket of dark ruby. Its resuscitating breath soaks into the warm purple carpet where the dawn dew hangs in the pearl clusters begging for a few seconds more of life in the splendour of their setting. The whole moorland is alive with colour, not harsh or garish, but subdued in tones that embrace the whole range of the spectrum.

'The interweaving patterns of heather contrast in purple hue through age, the new-born rich red fades

29

to a gentler tone in middle life and at old age takes on the complexion of old port. In between the heathers the burnt-out grass reflects the sunlight in burnished gold and isolated patches of whortleberries blaze scarlet against the brown. Away in the distance the granite-capped Tors now bathed in merciless light reflect back in blistering greys that sparkle and glitter in the brilliance.'

The solitude, the exhilaration and the freedom generated by walking on the Moor were truly expressed when Clive wrote movingly: 'I am alone, I am King. I have all this . . .'

Writers and painters, through the years, have come to the Moor, finding ideas and inspiration in the changing mood and colour. In what we foolishly call 'bad weather' these wide Dartmoor skies are dark and menacing like something from a horror film. In summer that Dartmoor blue haze gives everything a mellow quality. The Moor can produce a thousand images – and multiply them.

In the field of Art, Frederick John Widgery is accepted as the Prince of Dartmoor painters. He had a style all of his own, and though he died in 1942, he lives on in many moorland paintings and illustrations inside various books on Devon.

Cows grazing at Widecombe.

My Lady of the Moor

One building which must have mystified many visitors to Dartmoor for many years was a chapel at Venton – a chapel with a difference.

First, because a lamp was always burning inside the door and, more important, because it was basically built for just two people: an author, whose fiancé was killed in the war to end wars, and her mother. The girl never married, and some said she was never quite the same after her fiancé's death.

It stood improbably among old farm cottages with white walls and black rafters. The writer and her mother prayed there regularly – and any passers-by who wished to do the same were made welcome.

It is still there today – no longer a chapel but a memorial to a true Dartmoor eccentric.

Maybe the remoteness of the Moor works on people – more so probably in former generations before the motor car and television – days when journeys to places like Ashburton or Okehampton or Tavistock were real expeditions.

That brilliant Westcountry writer, the late Ronald Duncan, once said of Dartmoor, 'It is as if one had suddenly been transported on a time machine into a prehistoric world where cruelty was one dimension and loneliness the other dimension of man. I find I can easily believe the seventeenth-century description of the Moor: "wolves and winged serpents are no strangers to its hills and valleys . . ."'

Beatrice Chase was surely one of the most curious characters to live on the Moor. Her love affair with Dartmoor lasted more than half a century and her real

The Chapel at Venton.

name was Olive Katherine Parr; she and her mother came, at the beginning of the century, to live at Venton just outside the village of Widecombe.

Using the *nom de plume* Beatrice Chase, she began writing stories about Dartmoor and built up quite a following – *Through A Dartmoor Window* and *The Heart of the Moor* were among her best books. She skilfully portrayed people she knew such as Thirza Endacott, a neighbour, who attempted to commit suicide in an effort to 'lose' a curse which had been ill-wished upon her. She wrote too of a man, wearing an iron mask, concealing what was left of his face: the result of a shooting accident.

Outside her writing Beatrice Chase became positively eccentric. For years she played the role allotted to her in John Oxenham's novel *My Lady of the Moor* to the extent of accosting strangers, presenting them with a sprig of white heather and graciously 'giving' them the 'freedom' of the Moor!

There was something of King Arthur and the Court of Camelot in her make-up, for during the 1914–18 war, she began a crusade asking all men to lead clean lives. Those who wrote to her making such a promise, had their names written in a book which was lain before the altar in her chapel at Venton. Her Guild of 'White Knights' doubtless helped to increase her readership and fame. She also visited Dartmoor Prison and worked positively for reform in the prison system.

Ruth St Leger-Gordon in *Portrait of Devon* wrote: 'In spite of her idealism she was a lady very much disposed to take her own line, as I discovered upon our first personal acquaintance. Meeting far out on Dartmoor, and unkown to one another except by correspondence, she inquired the way to Cranmere Pool. I supplied the information, only to be told that it was incorrect according to her calculations. Her

Beatrice Chase's home.

imposing and resolute figure, as she strode off in the wrong direction, left an impression as indelible as it was mildly humorous.'

There was undoubtedly a mystical streak in her personality, and writing to Ruth St Leger-Gordon she sent an account of a strange personal experience. One summer day, at her Widecombe cottage, Beatrice Chase became aware of 'the cry' of the Dart which she said 'chilled and frightened her being an unusual sound at that time of the year'.

In the late 1920s gossip and rumour had it that Beatrice Chase was mentally ill. There was an alleged kidnapping in 1930 and at one stage even Scotland Yard were involved.

Sadly she did decline seriously in her latter years, when she insisted on keeping a gun for fear of intruders. She died on 3 July 1955 at the age of 80 in Newton Abbot Hospital.

A Roman Catholic, she claimed to be a direct descendant of Catherine Parr, the sixth wife of Henry VIII. She is buried in Widecombe Churchyard. On the margin of the graveyard near the famous old church are two granite crosses. One bears the inscription: 'Here lies Katharine Parr, Mother of Beatrice Chase who died in 1925.' The other says quite simply 'Pray for Olive Katharine Parr'.

She would surely have approved of this, her earthly resting place – looking across the Moors to the majestic and sometimes menacing tors and those wide Dartmoor skies.

'She is buried in Widecombe Churchyard.'

MDL-C

Kestor

Kestor rises to some 1452 feet on west Dartmoor, surmounted by a huge granite rock: an outstanding landmark that can be seen from miles around. The rock itself stands proud and alone, almost demanding that you climb to the top. Here will be found the mysterious rock basin, said to be the largest on Dartmoor, and generally filled with water.

It is indeed curious that this rock basin was only 'discovered' at the end of the last century, by the well-known Mr W. G. Ormerod, who found it full of turf. Perhaps the word 'discovered' is not altogether correct as we are sure this basin would have been in use centuries ago, possibly used by the old people in their ceremonies. One has the feeling of past rituals taking place here.

The rock basin was, at one time, surrounded by a railing, to protect animals from falling in, but this railing has long since rusted away.

From the top of the rock the view on a fine day is superb. Close at hand are the extensive remains of an old Iron Age settlement. It was here that the first evidence of metal working in Devon was found and Lady Aileen Fox, who supervised the excavation in 1951–52, put the date at around 400 BC. It was certainly a large settlement, as there were some 27 huts, with the largest of them known as 'Roundy Pound' which is where the iron smelting took place. There were both living and working quarters, suggesting the workers lived in, doubtless a self-contained group or family. Perhaps even in those days they wished to avoid industrial espionage. Even so, with its large well-defined fields and clear roads, this was an agricultural community.

One story we were told was how two old Chagford worthies walked out to Kestor one hot summer's day, and saw an adder on Kestor. One of the men drew an imaginary circle around the adder with his stick, and to the astonishment of the others, the adder seemed to be unable to get out – a true piece of Dartmoor folklore we think.

In the distance stands the fourteen foot figure of the 'Longstone' a tall majestic granite post, seemingly without any purpose. However, this mystery can be

Two views of Kestor.

The winter face of Kestor.

solved as this is the boundary stone of the Chagford, Gidleigh and Lydford parishes, and the site of many village revels in days gone by.

Mary Lou North, who lives at Batworthy Farm, Kestor Rock, near Chagford has been on Dartmoor since 1973. Though only in her twenties, she is wise and perceptive in her response to the terrain.

'I find Dartmoor a very challenging landscape,' she reflects, 'as its qualities are elusive and difficult to capture with the camera. It relies very much on lighting conditions and the weather to bring out atmosphere and the many moods of the Moor. Late autumn and winter months are my favourite times because of the low-angled light which picks out the subtleties of the scene. Bright sunny days transform the landscape into a flat featureless expanse.

'I am usually attracted to features on the Moor: walls, stones, man-made settlements, ruins, using them to lead into a picture or define it in some way. Sometimes the features are enough in themselves . . . like Wistman's Wood.

'Features such as quarries, houses, I find incongruous, but they also give a sense of history, a scale of time in the picture. Also without actually showing a human being, these man-made features give an indication of man in the landscape.'

The Longstone.

Spinsters' Rock

One of our favourite Devon characters is Spinsters' Rock, the only perfect cromlech in the whole country. It stands, as it has done since the megalithic period of prehistory, in a field between Drewsteignton and the lovely old stannary town of Chagford.

Some say the rock stands on a ley line linking Drewsteignton Church and Throwleigh. Once we touch the subject of ley lines we immediately enter a field of intriguing speculation and possibility – indeed certain students would put it more strongly, for more and more people are convinced these leys are genuinely psychic power centres.

Dr Joseph Heinsch, a celebrated German ley hunter, discovered that many sites of pagan ceremony and ancient trackways appeared to link up geometrically. Often the deep-thinking German Doctor reckoned that Holy lines radiated out from the hills, and churches were built on these lines because of a strong spiritual power.

How this ancient construction got here is another Devon mystery – over the years it has generated various theories. Spinsters' three sturdy upright slabs, seven feet in height, support a huge capping stone – and sturdy they must be for that stone is said to weigh as much as seventeen tons.

Folklore has it that three spinsters – not single ladies but spinners of yarn – one day spotted stones lying around, and being methodical folk, they gathered up the stones and erected this splendid cromlech. But one supposes that can only be half the story. Surely some Supernatural help was needed to get these massive stones into position.

A second version is that the word 'Spinsters' is a Gaelic corruption meaning a star-gazing place. While a third theory is the stones were carried here by a Moor man, and his three strong sons.

In its time it has been called the Drewsteignton or Shilston Cromlech, and has attracted many visitors.

But, at least, we know it is a megalithic burial chamber erected in the second millenium BC.

Bradford Pool

Just a short walk across the road from Spinsters' Rock and little known, are disused mine workings known as Bradford or Bradmere Pool.

Water is often linked to legend. But curiously here at Bradford Pool there is no legendary tale. There is, however, a mysterious quality about the place – the water covers as much as four acres – an almost hypnotic quality, it has been the scene of one suicide. It might, in fact, be a setting for a Tarzan or 'Sanders of the River' film for the big screen.

The mine here had a chequered career. The Civil War caused it to close down. It later was the subject of litigation – the case beginning in 1698 and apparently occupying the Courts for five long costly

Page 41, left and below: **'Mary Lou North's photography captures the strange beauty and quiet of this little known stretch of water.'**

years. There was a re-opening in 1782, but it finally closed, like so many mines, sadly and abruptly.

The pumps came to a halt, the continual ingress of water went unchecked and Bradford Pool, as it is known today, was formed. Mary Lou North's photography captures the strange beauty and quiet of this little known stretch of water.

The Devil's Stone at Shebbear

The village of Shebbear near the River Torridge stands in some of the most beautiful unspoilt countryside in North West Devon.

When bonfires light the skies of Devon each Guy Fawkes night, a curious old custom takes place here in the square at Shebbear. The Devil's Stone, weighing a ton, is set beneath an aged oak, and the ceremony of turning over the stone is performed annually by local bell ringers, using crow bars.

Some say the Devil himself was buried beneath the stone. Others say the act of turning 'his' stone ensures that he's kept away from the village for another year. The ritual is performed, after a religious ceremony and jangling of bells around it; generations of Shebbear men have kept up the tradition – and maybe for a good reason.

One November, during the 1914–18 War the stone was not turned, and the following calendar proved a disaster for the village: the harvest failed drastically, a high percentage of local men in the Services lost their lives – and old folk muttered darkly about 'The works of the Devil . . .' So perhaps it's wise the tradition is now maintained religiously each fifth evening in November.

But how the stone got its Satanic label remains a Devon mystery. The most popular legend is the Devil dropped it on his way to Hell, having been cast out of Heaven.

Right: '. . . the ceremony of turning over the stone . . .'

45

Left: **The Froude-Hancock Stone. A memorial to Squire Hancock of Rhyll Manor, the two names on the Stone commemorate his forbears, William Hancock and Mary Froude, daughter of the Vicar of Knowstone.**

William and Mary were married in 1806. He had a brewery in Taunton, was in the local yeomanry, had a shop and was generally a very busy man. He lived at Wiveliscombe. Only subsequently did his descendants move to Rhyll.

The Stone weighs 13 tons and according to S H Burton's *Exmoor*. . . was placed there in 1935 . . . brought from Marsh Bridge on a steam lorry.'

The 'Guardian' of the Valley of the Rocks.

Valley of Rocks

At this point in our journey we veered northward – and with good reason.

Some of the most mysterious shapes in all Devon are to be found in that strange eerie landscape, the Valley of Rocks on the North Devon coast, just a mile from Lynmouth.

Beatrix Cresswell, in an old guide on Barnstaple and the beauties of North Devon wrote '. . . save that they are not granite, the impression given by these rocks is that a bit of Dartmoor has dropped into Exmoor by the sea. The same impression of the frozen wave prevails.'

The poet Robert Southey was inspired by this impressive amphitheatre: 'Imagine a narrow vale between two ridges of hills, somewhat steep; the southern hill turfed; the vale, which runs from east to west, covered with huge stones and fragments of stone among the fern that fills it; the northern ridge completely bare, excoriated of all turf and all soil, the very bones and skeletons of the earth; rock reeling

Left: '. . . a bit of Dartmoor dropped into Exmoor by the sea.' *Below:* **The Thinker, sometimes known as The Drummer or The Drinker.**

upon rock, stone piled upon stone, a huge terrific mass. I ascended, with some toil, the highest point; two large stones inclining on each other formed a rude portal on the summit.'

Michael Deering's recent photography, especially commissioned for *Mysteries in the Devon Landscape*, portrays the brilliant sculpture of Nature hereabouts.

In a certain light, near dusk you could swear the Valley is peopled by men and women and not just rocks. Maybe that isn't such a fanciful idea either, because according to legend they were once humans, turned to stone for some frivolous behaviour like dancing or hurling, on a Sunday.

These strange shapes that people the valley positively fire the imagination. The captions to Michael Deering's photographs confirm this very fact, for he didn't just see 'stones' – he saw other things as the captions suggest.

Here stands the Devil's Cheesewring – some folk thought, from the shape and position of the rocks, this could have been the site of an ancient temple. Here too, in R. D. Blackmore's imagination came Jan Ridd to visit Mother Meldrum in *Lorna Doone*, seeking advice about his love life.

It was on a Sunday in Lent that Jan paid his visit: 'The Valley,' he says 'is a green, rough-sided hollow, bending at the middle, touched with stone at either crest and dotted here and there with slabs in and out the brambles. On the right hand (Jan was travelling from Lynton) is an upward crag, called by some the "Castle", easy enough to scale, and giving great views of the Channel. Facing this from the inland

Right: **The Valley of The Rocks.** *Left:* **The Animals.**

side and the elbow of the valley, a queer old pile of rocks arises bold behind one another and quite enough to affright a man, if it only were ten times larger. This is called the "Devil's Cheesewring" or the "Devil's Cheese Knife", which means the same thing, as our fathers were used to eating their cheese from a scoop . . . but all the middle of the valley was a place to rest in; to sit and think that troubles were not, if we would not make them. To know the sea outside the hills, but never to behold it. Our home folk always call it the "Danes" or the "Denes" which is no more, they tell me, than a hollow place.'

The Hanging Stone, Combe Martin

Combe Martin on the north coast of Devon boasts one of the strangest houses in all England, an eighteenth-century inn. It's called the Pack of Cards, for the very good reason that it all goes back to one Squire Ley who was a highly successful gambler. The squire won a fortune at the gambling tables, and decided to keep his fame alive by building a kind of memorial to himself. The Pack of Cards is the result, reflecting the man and his gambling lifestyle – there are four storeys for the four suits and thirteen windows to each storey – though some were boarded up after his death in 1716 when the building changed its lifestyle and became an inn.

However, the reason for our visit to this northerly corner of Devon was a strange, mighty stone; the boundary mark of Combe Martin Parish. It is known as the Hanging Stone, and has a close relation on Dartmoor. Interestingly in each case virtually the same story is told to account for the curious name.

We are indebted again to fellow Bossiney author, Sally Jones, who introduced us to both the stone and the story. Here is Sally's account in *Legends of Devon*.

'A thief stole a sheep and tied it round his neck as the easiest way to carry it home. On the way back, he rested on a rock to try and get his breath back. Sadly for him, the reverse happened, for the sheep struggled and slid over the side, strangling him. The story is not restricted to this part of Devon for there are two other formations known as the Hangman's Stone, one in Sidmouth and one in Leicestershire – and each carries a similar legend to the one at Combe Martin.

'The fact that the legend is the same in each case points not so much to the same event occurring; that would seem too much of a coincidence, but to a common derivation of the names, the Saxon *stanes hengen* – hanging or uplifted stones. The legend is obviously intended to point out to any would-be thieves that crime doesn't pay, and it was probably put about by Christian moralists far more interested in ethics than etymology.'

The Hanging Stone by Felicity Young.

Around Hartland

In our exploration of North Devon, we were especially interested in the reputed hauntings of Saint Nectan in the Hartland area because St Nectan's Glen, near Bossiney, is rated one of the most haunted areas in the whole of the Westcountry.

The road, that runs alongside Hartland Abbey, and from there to the church, is said to be haunted by a ghostly procession.

We asked Antony D. Hippisley Coxe, author of *Haunted Britain*, whether he knew anyone thereabouts who had had Supernatural type experiences. He recalled how 'Billy Upton, who lived at Trellick opposite our house at Hartland, got pixie led and could not get out of a field. When I told him he should have "turned his coat" he gave me "the sideways look".

'Harold Lockyer, the Vicar of Hartland, now dead, told me he had seen Saint Nectan after putting away the chalice at Communion Service one day.

'After writing *Haunted Britain*, I heard that Bow Bridge, just east of Hartland Abbey, was haunted by two old ladies. A local girl, then Miss Dennis, and now Mrs Shadrick of Chilsworthy, told me she had seen a field "full of light".'

Two views of St Nectan's Church; the rare vertical sundial is shown in detail on the left.

Right: **Bow Bridge near Hartland said to be haunted by two old ladies.** *Left:* **The mysterious rocks by Hartland Quay.**

Literary Link at Manaton

Whenever we came through the Dartmoor village of Manaton we wonder how many visitors know the link between Manaton and the *Forsyte Saga* which was such a television success back in the 1960s.

The fact is that great literary work was conceived here on Dartmoor where its author John Galsworthy spent seventeen happy highly productive years. From 1906 to 1924 Galsworthy lived at Wingstone Farm, Manaton, as a plaque on the veranda confirms.

Bernard Shaw visited him here. No recluse, Galsworthy loved riding across the Moor on horseback, was a founder of the local rifle club, and became captain of Manaton Cricket Club. He played cricket for the village for seventeen summers – and his highest score was four runs – off an outside edge we've heard! Moreover the scorer, in error, put them down as four leg-byes.

He was awarded the Nobel Prize for Literature in 1932, and died in London the following year. The award naturally gave him great pleasure, but many local people felt he was happiest on Dartmoor, and never more so than when he was trying to trace his family tree back to the Moor. In a poem he wrote with feeling:

> *Moor of my name where the road leads high*
> *Through heather and bracken and gorse and grass.*

Galsworthy, great man of letters, the Manaton Edition of his work contains as many as thirty volumes, may be no mystery. But we suspect few who explore this Manaton-North Bovey area in the summer months are aware of his affection for the place – or the fact that he lived on this farm, and produced so much here.

John Galsworthy's farm near Manaton.

Ten Commandments

Finding the Ten Commandments, carved into two slabs of granite, in Devon may not be a mystery – more of a surprise – and a curious tale lies behind this extraordinary piece of craftsmanship.

Two men and a Parliamentary defeat were responsible for their being.

Furthermore Mary Lou North's photography of the Commandments is rare – one of the first we've seen on any published page.

It all goes back to the year 1928 when Mr Whitley, who lived at Welstor, asked Arthur Clement of Exmouth to carve the Ten Commandments to celebrate the defeat of the Revised Prayer Book of 1927-28.

Right and overleaf: **Rare photos of the Ten Commandments Stone.**

Arthur Clement accepted the commission and, in a way, it took him forty days and forty nights because during the daylight hours, he carved away on the top of Buckland Beacon, and at night he slept in a hayloft down in the woods, his bed rudely fashioned with wire netting for a mattress.

During the carving operation, Mr Whitley paid visits to the summit to inspect the work. He went up the easy way – on horseback, accompanied by several dogs. On one such ride he referred to Arthur as 'Moses', but the carver retorted: 'It is rather inappropriate, sir, as Moses carried the tablets of stone down to the Children of Israel, and I have no intention of doing that!'

The reverse was rather the case, for Mr Whitley had chosen the two granite rocks which were originally lying down on the lower slopes of the tor.

Anyway the Commandments remain: a memorial to a kind of eccentricity and a splendid grandstand from which to view this Devon landscape.

Bleak House

Did Charles Dickens ever come to Dartmoor?

If he did, he would have been intrigued to find a Bleak House there, near Rattlebrook.

This building, standing alone in the depths of the great Moor, was once occupied by a curious German chemist who worked long hours alone in his laboratory, making secret experiments. We can guess the kind of gossip the foreigner must have generated around the Dartmoor villages.

Mary Lou North's picture of Bleak House shows all that remains of the old building. The noise of labour and life died long ago.

Roger Alford, an expert moorman and local farmer, told us how the chemist finally and successfully arrived at a formula whereby he could produce alcohol from Dartmoor peat! But dramatically and to the chagrin of the speculators – the men who had backed him financially – the chemist died, taking his secret formula with him to the grave. Not a scrap of paper relating to the formula could be found anywhere in the house or the laboratory.

A curious little tale proving that fact can indeed be stranger than fiction.

Overleaf: Bleak House.

The Ice Works

High up on Sourton Tors is a most unusual series of seemingly large grass steps. To an imaginative Dartmoor walker or hiker these might look as though they belonged to some giant from the Moor's misty past – a mystery to be solved? Really more a curiosity for there is a rational explanation for these 'steps'.

They were not formed by some quirk of nature, or some geological freak; they were deliberately made by man for a simple manufacturing purpose. More than a hundred years ago – back in the 1870s – some speculators hit upon the novel idea of 'manufacturing' ice here on the Moor. Where better than Sourton

All that remains of where the ice was stored.

Tors, they reasoned, with its ready spring and high rain fall.

The steps we see today, were the result of a great deal of hard work. The large containers, where the ice was stored in the bleak winter months, were perfectly situated. Bracken was placed on top to give insulation and to prevent thawing when the warmer weather arrived.

The speculators looked to Plymouth for their business success. The flourishing fleet of fishermen at Plymouth had a readymade market in the high class hotels of the city, and ice was a necessary part of that business. Horse-drawn carts, carrying ice, became a familiar sight on the road through Tavistock and Yelverton on their way to Plymouth.

But sadly the operators never completely solved the problem of ice melting on that journey. Consequently profits were lost and the industry only lasted a few years. With the benefit of hindsight, the venture stood very little chance of economic success. But the remains of the ice factory at Sourton stand as a curious memorial to a curious enterprise.

Loaf and Cheese

The explanation of the Ice Works may be quite simple and rational, but the mystery of the two large boulders, known as Branscombe's Loaf and Cheese on the plateau-like summit of the rock strewn Cornridge, is not. Here there is a story truly in keeping with the mystery and folklore of Dartmoor.

Once again Roger Alford has been of help. It all started some 700 years ago in the thirteenth century when the redoubtable Walter Branscombe was the Bishop of Exeter. Covering a wide and scattered area with a great deal of Dartmoor within his 'parish' it was one of the most difficult, taxing jobs for any clergyman in the country.

Beset by all the difficulties involved in communication and travelling in those days, and especially the arduous journeys in bad weather, the Bishop never-theless made regular visits to his moorland clergy. He travelled on horseback. It was on one of these visits that the Bishop accompanied only by his trusty manservant, was making his way back to Exeter, and was crossing below the Cornridge, possibly somewhere above where the Okehampton-Tavistock road stands today.

Tired and in need of rest and refreshment the Bishop encountered a stranger who thoughtfully offered them some sustenance. The stranger then produced from his bag a small round loaf and a lump of cheese which the Bishop gratefully received and was about to partake, when there was a sudden cry

Right: **Branscombe's Loaf and Cheese.**

64

from the servant as he struck the food from the Bishop's hand. Apparently the servant, glancing down at the feet of the stranger, noticed he was not wearing boots or shoes but, instead, cloven hooves protruded from beneath the travelling cloak! The Bishop had nearly partaken of food with the Devil.

Folklore has it that both loaf and cheese flew in different directions, but both landed in the Corn-ridge, where they were converted into two large granite boulders and even today they are known as Branscombe's Loaf and Cheese.

A far-fetched tale, the twentieth-century cynic will say, but we wonder whether there can really be smoke without fire even among the folklore of wild Dartmoor.

Does Bishop Branscombe's ghost haunt these parts, recalling the day he encountered the Devil himself?

Bathe Pool

At Bathe Farm, North Tawton, there is a great hollow which generally is completely empty, and is strangely known as Bathe Pool.

Legend dating from the time of the first Elizabeth has it that when the pool floods, it heralds the death of a member of the Royal Family, or the beginning of a war. The quotation, attributed to an unnamed Privy Councillor, of that first Elizabeth, is: 'Which over-floweth before the death of any great prince or strange occurrence of great importance.' Certainly evidence appears to confirm that tradition because the Pool was full in the following years.

Bathe Pool near Tawton.

1805 The deaths of Admiral Nelson and William Pitt.
1817 Death of Princess Charlotte.
1852 Death of the Duke of Wellington.
1910 Death of Edward VIII.
1914 The outbreak of the first World War.

During our research into this odd tradition, two interesting coincidences appeared, both connected with the medical profession. First, when the pool overflows, the cellar of the house, for many years used by the local doctor at North Tawton, floods, and secondly, this farm was where Dr William Budd – a subject in *Curiosities of Devon* – first conducted his research into the transmission of the bacillus of typhoid fever in 1839, work that was to make him a famous man of medicine.

White Rock, Sticklepath

Poundsgate Methodist Church — only open on the first Sunday in the month.

The many Methodist chapels scattered over the Devon landscape are vivid reminders of John Wesley's visits to the Westcountry – and the power of his preaching.

But it is not always a man-made building that reminds us, and Sticklepath is such a case. As you journey in the direction of Cornwall, and begin the steep climb out of the village, a large white rock and flag pole stand prominently high above the left-hand side of the road.

Wesley made a number of visits to the village, and this rock became his open-air pulpit. On occasions, the preacher on horseback encountered fierce hostility in the Westcountry, but he remembered his first visit to Sticklepath with affection. Writing in his *Journal* on 22 September 1743, he recorded:

'As we were riding through a village called Sticklepath, one stopped me in the street and asked abruptly, "Is not thy name John Wesley?" Immediately two or three more came up, and told me I must stop there. I did so; and before we had spoken many words, our souls took acquaintance with each other. I found they were called Quakers: but that hurt not me; seeing the love of God was in their hearts.'

Wesley's sheer physical achievements were enormous. He rode over 250,000 miles, sometimes covering 70 miles and delivering three sermons in the same day – initially many of them before hostile gather-

Left: **John Wesley, carved by Burnard, the brilliant Cornish sculptor of the 1800s. To see this splendid carving, you will need to cross the Tamar. Wesley's head stands proudly above the door of an old building in Altarnun village on the edge of Bodmin Moor where Burnard was born in 1818.**
Right: **View from White Rock, Sticklepath.**

ings, with eggs and stones thrown at him. He wrote 233 original works, including a four-volume history of England, earning £40,000 in royalties and giving every penny away.

Outside and beyond all this, he set up a free medical dispensary, adapted an electrical machine for healing, opened spinning and knitting shops for the poor, and not only founded the Kingswood School for boys but wrote the text books as well.

The white rock of Sticklepath, in its modest way, is an eloquent epitaph to this great Non-Conformist Crusader.

From such stones, the fires of Methodism were kindled.

Tom Pearse?

It is rare – indeed it is almost certainly a contradiction to say you've come face to face with a legend. But we have encountered a legend, or at least, part of one on this journey.

Folklore in Devon is nearly as rich as its clotted cream, and the story of Tom Pearse's grey mare is probably one of the most famous. As animal lovers, we don't particularly like the story, but the tale of Tom Pearse's old grey mare carrying a team of thoughtless men to Widecombe Fair is now part of Devon's tapestry. Inevitably their collective weight proved too much for the animal, and she 'took sick and died'.

According to an old ballad they haunt the Moor in a group:

When the wind whistles cold on the moor of a night,
All along, down along, out along, lee,
Tom Pearse's old mare doth appear ghastly white,
Wi' Bill Brewer, Jan Stewer, Peter Gurney,
Peter Davy, Dan'l Whiddon, Harry Hawk,
Old Uncle Tom Cobbleigh and all.

However we have met no-one who claims to have seen the ghostly group. But we have stood outside a stable which some say once housed the unfortunate grey mare. The small granite stable stands hard by the old mill at Sticklepath. Investigations reveal that a Bill Brewer did, in fact, live in Sticklepath, and the much respected Pearse family operated the local mill for something like three decades – they were great

Right: **The stable at Sticklepath. Was Tom Pearse's grey mare stabled here?**

70

benefactors to the village – and, above all, there was a Tom Pearse in the family.

Doubtless a man of his position would have owned a horse – and where better to keep it: close to the mill itself? In our imagination, we can picture the possible leg-pulling among the locals. 'Let's go to Widecombe Fair?' 'How shall we get there?' 'The boss's horse? Who will ask?'

And perhaps finally 'Tom Pearse, Tom Pearse, lend me they grey mare?'

Lydford

Lydford can attract you for various reasons: the castle or the church – the church was here before the castle – or the gorge or the inn.

Arthur Mee, on his visit, referred to 'the eerie enchantment of its wooded gorge . . . in the deep dark chasm where the Lydd swirls like a witch's cauldron in its rocky bed.'

We came to Lydford for another reason.

Graveyards are fascinating places, and here at Lydford we found surely one of the most curious epitaphs in any Devon churchyard.

Right: **The rural scene, which William Browne loved so much.**
Far right: **A curious epitaph.**

...

In ...
... ...
... ...
... ...
... ...
That he never went wrong
Except when set agoing
By people
Who did not know
his key
Even then he was easily
Set right again
He had the art of disposing his time
So well
That his hours glided away
In one continual round
Of pleasure and delight
Till an unlucky minute put a period to
His existence
He departed this Life
Nov.r 14 1802
Aged 57
Wound up
In hopes of being taken in hand
By his Maker
And of being thoroughly cleaned repaired
And Set a going
In the World to come

Here lies in horizontal position
The outsize case of
GEORGE ROUTLEDGE, Watchmaker
Whose abilities in that line were an honour
To his profession
Integrity was the mainspring,
And prudence the regulator
Of all the actions of his life.
Human, generous and liberal
His hand never stopped
Till he had relieved distress.
So much regulated were all his motions
That he never went wrong
Except when set agoing
By people
Who did not know
His key.
Even then he was easily
Set right again.
He had the art of disposing his time
So well
That his hours glided away
In one continual round
Of pleasure and delight
Till an unlucky minute put a period to
His existence.
He departed this life
Nov. 14 ..1802
Aged 57
Wound up
In hopes of being taken in hand
By his Maker
And of being thoroughly cleaned, repaired
And set-going
In the world to come

Below: **The Watchmaker's Tomb at Lydford.** *Right:* **Lydford Castle built in 1195.**

Lydford Castle. 'Terrible deeds took place inside these walls.'

But having come here it would be criminal not to visit the castle and the gorge.

The castle, built in 1195, was used to house offenders against the stannary tin laws, and some terrible deeds took place inside these ancient walls. It was once described as 'one of the most hideous, contagious and detestable places in the realm'.

This stannary court had such a reputation that the Devon poet William Browne was moved to write:

I've oftimes heard of Lydford Law
How in the morn they hang and draw,
And sit in judgement after.

Browne, who was born at Tavistock in 1591, was educated at Tavistock Grammar School, and later at Exeter College, Oxford. Well known and well liked, he had as contemporaries Ben Jonson and Michael Drayton. He loved the rural scene and his greatest work *Brittania's Pastorals* was published in three books. Famous characters like Milton and Keats admitted they owed a debt to this son of Devon.

Judge Jeffreys presided at Lydford and is said to haunt the place. There is undeniably an eerie atmosphere and fairly recently we heard of a teacher with a party of schoolchildren being overcome from a feeling of evil and having to rush away.

Oddly enough, though a popular beauty spot, Lydford Gorge has been the scene of many suicides. Is there something in the atmosphere here that drives a despairing person to that final terrible act?

Lydford Gorge.

Dartmoor, covering 365 square miles, has relatively few trees. Here are two of them, one down but still alive, both telling us trees have personalities of their own, reminding us too that Dartmoor remains essentially a mysterious landscape.

Some of the Dartmoor stone walling has a magnificently sculptural quality, and in a way that's profoundly true, for the man who built this was surely a kind of sculptor. How long ago did he do it? Who was he? Aspects of the terrain trigger questions, firing your curiosity and imagination.

Tolmen

Healing stones were once treated seriously. One such stone is here in Devon, situated in the North Teign River on Dartmoor. Known as the Tolmen – tol means hole, and maen means stone – it is a huge boulder in the river bed. One assumes the hole has been worn through by friction over the passage of time. Those who climb on to the rock and slide through on to the stone slab beneath are cured of all rheumatic ailments – that anyway is what the old folk believed.

It has a Cornish counterpart, down in the Hundred of Penwith: the Men-an-Tol – meaning the stone of the hole – through which generations of sick Cornish adults and children either crawled or were pulled or pushed, all in the belief that a cure would take place.

Janet and Colin Bord in their fine book *The Secret Country* devoted a whole chapter to stones and their powers. 'It would seem,' they wrote, 'as if the hidden current which flows through the land can be tapped at certain points, much as an electric socket on the skirting board of our sitting room enables us to "plug in" to the current and put it to use.'

Fitz's Well

High above Okehampton on Dartmoor stands a stone cross known as Fitz's Well.

Various stories relate to this place. Two have a link with the nearby Artillery Camp. Time was – before the coming of the motor car – when a soldier on horseback went each morning and evening down into the town of Okehampton, to deliver and collect mail from the town post office. One misty morning the soldier, on mail duty, saddled his horse and made his way down to the post office, where all the incoming mail was placed in the saddlebags. Horse and rider were last seen on the steep hill making their way back to camp. Neither were ever seen again, and some old folk maintained the cross marked their grave, both having been swallowed in the murky depths.

Another variation is that a gun carriage, complete with horses, was lost in the surrounding bog. But there is no historical evidence to support either story.

According to local folklore if a person is lost on the

Right: **The Tolmen.**

Hilary Wreford talking to Dartmoor Ranger Eddie Hain
at Fitz's Well near Okehampton.

Moor or has been pixie led, he or she has only to drink of Fitz's Well, and they will recover their bearings – and get home safely. The cynics though say, 'Once you get here, you're on the edge of the Moor anyway and help is usually at hand.'

Another local tradition is that any young unmarried woman seeking a suitable husband found him by simply drinking from Fitz's Well early in the morning on Easter Day. By doing precisely that, they believed she would marry within the year. Alas the tradition is more difficult to test nowadays, for any young lady will find the well covered in large granite stones.

This well near Okehampton and another near Princetown both owe their name to Sir John Fitz who was a Lord of the Manor on Dartmoor in the sixteenth century.

Roman Chair

You will find the Roman Chair high up on Halstock, near Okehampton, on the side of a valley facing a cluster of rocks known as Belstone Cleave.

It may have an air of mystery, but this large protruding granite is shaped like a giant's chair – indeed *is* a chair – for one of us has sat in it. Mary Lou's photograph is a rarity, and she obtained it one Friday afternoon when we struggled through tangled bushes and gorse to the site.

Some of the old folk believed this chair had been fashioned by Romans using crude tools of their day. It is also thought Julius Caesar, with soldiers, camped at Lydford less than a day's ride away. The camp or fort here at Halstock is thought to be Roman – so it may really be a Roman chair.

But others say Dartmoor pixies carried out the carving, and others more cynically say 'the chair' has been shaped by the weathering of many centuries. Either way, it remains a real Devon mystery and curiosity and known only to a tiny percentage of people who tour these parts.

Overleaf: **Hilary Wreford at the Roman Chair, Halstock.**

Halstock Chapel

It is surprising that in our travels we have come across some mysterious object, only to find others in close proximity, sometimes with no direct connection. Here was such a case. After we had visited the site of the Iron Age fort we left the 'Roman Chair' and trekked to an area known as 'Chapel Lands', where in the corner of the field once stood the Chapel of St Michael of Halstock. Yet so faint and scattered are the remains, that the average walker might pass and be unaware that this place of worship once existed hereabouts.

This chapel was probably first used in Saxon times and although the history of this place is clouded in the mysteries of distant time, it was no doubt of importance. Sadly this ancient place of worship has been left at the mercy of the elements and only the outline of the building can be seen today. There was, it seems, more than a chapel as traces of other buildings can be identified, and it is said once there was a village of Halstock, even equipped with its own hospital, though everything is now overgrown.

Legend also has it that there was an underground passage connecting Okehampton Castle and Halstock but this would have been a long, difficult construction, and we feel sure that there is little foundation in the theory.

Although we were reluctant to leave this enchanting spot, we wanted to examine the two cave-like openings on the west side of the River Ockment. Not the home of some prehistoric animals, they were the entrances to the old Halstock Mine, sometimes known as Halestock Mine or simply Wheal Castle. We crossed the river to examine the dark menacing apertures, and found that one shaft did not extend far into the hillside, but the other went deeper, and the main shaft is submersed in water, completely impossible to enter. Unfortunately, there are few records of this mine. Apparently some considerable amounts of copper were extracted as well as other minerals. However, it closed one hundred years ago, and has just been left to die. You can imagine the miners making their way to work over the rugged terrain from the neighbouring villages in all weathers.

As we were leaving we made a surprise discovery; the site of a Dartmoor letterbox. Underneath a stone slab were all the necessary ingredients contained in a tin – a visitor's book, pen, stamp pad and, of course, the stamp itself which proclaimed 'The Wheal Castle Mine'. Perhaps it would be remiss if we did not mention the growing industry of 'Dartmoor Letterboxes'. Certainly they are not of the red-coated type which we use for everyday mail. These Dartmoor containers of all shapes and sizes, some temporary, others permanent, have sprung up over the Moor since 1854, when the first 'box' was placed at Cranmere Pool, the home of the legendary Benji Gayer whose ghost is still said to haunt the Pool. There are now thought to be over 400 letterboxes on the Moor.

Right: **Entrance to the old mine at Halstock.**

Left: **The grounds of Halstock Chapel.**

Splinterproof

Splinterproof is a word that has mystified many a Dartmoor visitor. You will find no reference to it in most guide books. However, the word is known to the military and the locals. It describes the granite-built enclosures, constructed as observation posts to report on and direct the artillery fire during army training.

Our photograph shows observation post No. 14, high on Dartmoor, where we interviewed Mr Alfie Sanders, the only person still living who worked on the construction of the Splinterproof. He was in fine form as he enjoyed recollecting the old days. Alfie, now retired, was a creative mason, and always enjoyed the hard work of fashioning granite. He worked on many projects on Dartmoor, including all the Splinterproofs, and he was quick to remind us that the correct name for No. 14 was 'Blackavon Spur'. The original Splinterproofs were actually built on timber bulks but in 1925 the military embarked on a programme of replacing these with the robust granite shapes we see today.

Alfie told us many curious tales of the Moor, including how he went to Dinger Tor to work one misty morning, only to find a housemaid from a neighbouring town sitting on a stone near the top, after getting lost in the mist, while taking a quiet stroll the previous afternoon! He could even laugh at himself as he recounted that, with a number of other tradesmen, he was making his way from Yes Tor to High Willhayes when a thick mist descended. Anyway they carried on walking, and, when the mist cleared, they discovered they had only succeeded in walking round Yes Tor three times finishing up in much the same spot!

Grimspound

Our visit to Grimspound, we felt, was the next best thing to travelling on a time machine. Once there, we felt we needed the company of Shirley Wallis – with her gift of travelling back in time.

Here she would have needed to travel a long way, for Grimspound is all that remains of an Early Bronze Age village. Grimspound spreads itself over something like four acres, comprising the remains of 24

Right: **Splinterproof no 14.**

Left: **Sabine Baring-Gould photographed by Robert Burnard in 1894.** *Right:* **Grimspound.**

hut circles. Some say that as many as 1,400 hut circles are scattered over the Moor.

Standing here you realise time is a curious thing. You feel that veil separating the here and now and the distant past can seem strangely thin. It is almost as if the echoes of the long ago send a shiver across the Dartmoor of today.

We handled the slabs of grey granite and wondered if visitors of former generations were right when they ascribed magical qualities to them.

The thoughtful Ronald Duncan probably got to the heart of the matter, when he reflected: 'At one time, the Moor had a great number of pagan religious structures, similar no doubt to Stonehenge and Avebury. But most of these antiquities were either demolished by the Christians, who used the granite

to build their own churches as at Chagford, or they were carted off to be used for farmhouse lintels, gateposts or bridges. But enough remain as at Grimspound to show that the Moor was once a place like Salisbury Plain, of particular religious significance – no doubt because it was high ground.'

Ninety years span our photographs of Grimspound. Three were taken by Mary Lou North in May 1985, and the fifth of Sabine Baring-Gould by Robert Burnard in May 1894.

The two men supervised the excavation of these 24 huts at Grimspound in 1896. Baring-Gould, squire and parson at Lewtrenchard, wrote among many other things, those splendidly stirring hymns *Now The Day Is Over* and *Onward Christian Soldiers*. Robert Burnard was a gifted amateur photographer and the

first man to suggest the conservation solution of Dartmoor by advocating a national park. He was for many years Secretary of the Dartmoor Preservation Society and died in 1920.

Baring-Gould, too, was passionately concerned about preserving the Moor and was a founder member of the Association.

If we were pressed to select just one place which truly personifies the soul of Mysterious Devon, we would choose Grimspound.

But for compiling this book we may not have come here. We are therefore grateful Grimspound compelled us to come. There is no finer place to finish a journey among the mysteries in the Devon landscape.

Here you somehow find yourself on the edge of civilization.

Below and right: **Grimspound. 'There is no finer place to finish a journey among the mysteries in the Devon landscape.'**

PLATE ACKNOWLEDGMENTS

Front cover by Ray Bishop — Maggie Ginger riding
Meridian at Hound Tor.
Back cover by Mary Lou North — Wistman's Wood.

Mary Lou North: pages 5-8, 12-14, 18, 19, 24, 34-38, 41-43, 59-65, 69, 71, 73-77, 81-89, 91-93
Ray Bishop: pages 10, 16, 20, 21, 23, 28-33, 58, 67, 68, 72, 78, 79
Michael Deering: pages 9, 11, 46-50, 54-57
Felicity Young: pages 17, 26, 39, 53
Roy Westlake: page 51
Waverley Photographic: page 45
Robert Burnard: page 90
By courtesy of John Shields: page 66

ACKNOWLEDGMENTS

Both authors wish to thank all those who have helped with pictures and information; the Westcountry Studies Library at Exeter whose staff have been most helpful on this and other occasions; Michael Wreford for reading, talking, listening, driving and walking; Maggie Ginger and her mare Meridian for appearing on the cover and in some of the Dartmoor photographs — and Maggie for her skills of design in this and so many Bossiney titles — and not least Brenda Duxbury and Angela Thomas for their editorial work. This then is essentially a team effort.

Also available

DARTMOOR IN THE OLD DAYS

by James Mildren. 145 photographs.

James Mildren is an author who is at home in the wilderness of his Dartmoor.

'Lovers of Dartmoor will need no persuasion to obtain a copy. To anybody else, I suggest they give it a try. It may lead to a better understanding of why many people want Dartmoor to remain a wonderful wilderness.'

Keith Whitford, The Western

125 YEARS WITH THE WESTERN MORNING NEWS

by James Mildren. 150 photographs.

Stories and photographs that have made the headlines in the Westcountry since the paper's birth in 1860.

'James Mildren's splendid 125 year illustrated survey. His unobtrusive presence is a model for all historians.'

Express and Echo

AROUND GLORIOUS DEVON

by David Young. 148 photographs.

David Young, well known in the Westcountry as TSW's roving architect, takes us on a personally-conducted tour of his glorious Devon.

'. . . proves as good a guide in print as he is on the small screen.'

Judy Diss, Herald Express

VIEWS OF OLD DEVON

Rosemary Anne Lauder provides the text for more than 200 old postcards, evocative of a world and a way of life that has gone. Words and pictures combine to produce a book that will delight all who love Devon.

'Only the camera can turn back the clock like this.'

The Sunday Independent

VIEWS OF OLD PLYMOUTH

by Sarah Foot

Words and old pictures combine to recall Plymouth as it once was: a reminder of those great times past and of the spirit of the people of Plymouth.

'This is a lovely nostalgia-ridden book and one which no real Plymothian will want to be without.'

James Mildren, The Western Morning News

THE CORNISH COUNTRYSIDE

by Sarah Foot. 130 illustrations, 40 in colour.

Here, in Bossiney's first colour publication, Sarah Foot explores inland Cornwall, the moors and the valleys, and meets those who work on the land.

'Sarah Foot sets out to share her obvious passion for Cornwall and to describe its enigmas . . . It is a book for those who are already in love with Cornwall and for those who would like to know her better.'

Alison Foster, The Cornish Times

EXMOOR IN THE OLD DAYS

by Rosemary Anne Lauder. 147 old photographs.

The author perceptively shows that Exmoor is not only the most beautiful of our Westcountry moors but is also rich in history and character: a world of its own in fact.

'. . . contains scores of old photographs and picture postcards . . . will provide a passport for many trips down memory lane . . .'

Bideford Gazette

RIVERS OF CORNWALL

by Sarah Foot. 130 photographs, 45 in colour.

The author explores six great Cornish rivers: the Helford, the Fal, the Fowey, the Camel, the Lynher and the Tamar.

'. . . makes use of many colour illustrations as well as black and white and shows that whatever changes may have taken place in the river economics they remain places of quality and beauty, quintessentially Cornwall.'

The Cornish Guardian

100 YEAR ON BODMIN MOOR

by E.V. Thompson

A rich harvest of old photographs and picture postcards, reflecting life on the Moor for a century with a perceptive text.

'. . . will entice the present day visitor to Cornwall to explore the Moor . . .'

Pamela Luke, The Methodist Recorder

SOMERSET IN THE OLD DAYS

by David Young. 145 old photographs.

David Young of TSW takes a journey in words and old pictures across Somerset.

'. . . a rich harvest of old Somerset photographs.'

Somerset and Avon Life

OTHER BOSSINEY TITLES INCLUDE:

LEGENDS OF DEVON
by Sally Jones

GHOSTS OF DEVON
by Peter Underwood

STRANGE STORES FROM DEVON
by Rosemary Anne Lauder and Michael Williams

SEA STORIES OF DEVON
introduced by E.V.Thompson

DARTMOOR PRISON
by Rufus Endle

HEALING HARMONY AND HEALTH
by Barney Camfield

UNKNOWN SOMERSET
by Rosemary Clinch and Michael Williams

UNKNOWN BRISTOL
by Rosemary Clinch

WESTCOUNTRY MYSTERIES
introduced by Colin Wilson

CURIOSITIES OF SOMERSET
by Lornie Leete-Hodge

NORTH CORNWALL IN THE OLD DAYS
by Joan Rendell

AROUND BUDE AND STRATTON
by Joan Rendell

100 YEARS AROUND THE LIZARD
by Jean Stubbs

MOUNT'S BAY
by Douglas Williams

VIEWS OF OLD CORNWALL
by Sarah Foot

CURIOSITIES OF DEVON
by Michael Williams

DEVON MYSTERIES
by Judy Chard

STRANGE SOMERSET STORIES
introduced by David Foot

SEA STORIES OF CORNWALL
by Ken Duxbury

POLDARK COUNTRY
by David Clarke

KING ARTHUR COUNTRY IN CORNWALL
by Brenda Duxbury, Michael Williams and Colin Wilson

DISCOVERING BODMIN MOOR
by E.V. Thompson

LEGENDS OF CORNWALL
by Sally Jones

GHOSTS OF CORNWALL
by Peter Underwood

SUPERSTITION AND FOLKLORE
by Michael Williams

CRUEL CORNISH SEA
by David Mudd

AROUND AND ABOUT THE ROSELAND
by David Mudd

MY DEVON
by Hugh Caradon, Judy Chard, Andrew Cooper, Robin Davidson, Daniel Farson, Sarah Foot, Clive Gunnell, James Mildren, Mary and Hal Price.

We shall be pleased to send our catalogue giving full details of our growing list of titles for Devon, Cornwall and Somerset and forthcoming publications.

If you have difficulty in obtaining our titles, write direct to Bossiney Books, Land's End, St Teath, Bodmin, Cornwall.